Wishing stone stories
Stage 9

Name

Practise your handwriting.

'Let's make a wish on the magic stone,'

said Yasmin, and she held out in her hand a little stone.

It was pink and grey and blue and in the middle was a hole.

Lee put his finger in the hole. Then they all shut their eyes

and whispered, 'One ... two ... three ... wish-sh-sh-sh.'

Adventure at sea

Skill: Practising neat handwriting
Instructions: Read the passage through them copy it out in your neatest handwriting.

Join the word to the rhyming picture.

The _____ little dog _____ its paw.   (cut cute)

Look at the _____ through the window _____.   (pan pane)

_____ the skin from the _____ pear.   (rip ripe)

I _____ you can _____.   (hop hope)

Adventure at sea

Skill: Phonological awareness – long and short vowels
Instructions: Join the word to its rhyming picture. Then complete the sentences using the correct words.

Write the speech.

1

'I wish we could see what it's like down under the molehill,' said Lee.

2

'We would like to have a look around your home,' said Yasmin.

3 It's a baby Tyrannosaurus!

4 It's got very big teeth.

Journey into the earth

Skill: Identifying speech and using speech bubbles
Instructions: In 1 and 2 fill in the speech bubbles with the direct speech. In 3 and 4 write the direct speech as reported speech. Remind the children where to put the speech marks.

Sequence the story.

__1__ Yasmin, Jack and Lee were in a long dark tunnel. They saw a mole.

___ Just then a fox's nose came pushing down the tunnel.

___ Soon there was a big wall right across the tunnel.

___ So the children followed the mole. Then the mole stopped. 'I can smell a fox,' he said.

___ 'The wall will not stop the fox for long,' said the mole, and he began to dig a new tunnel.

___ 'Hello,' said the mole. 'This tunnel is my home. Follow me.'

___ 'We must all make a wall to keep out the fox,' said the mole.

___ The mole dug the new tunnel as fast as he could.

___ So they all began to dig as hard as they could.

___ He dug so quickly that soon the children could not see him.

Journey into the earth

Skill: Reading for meaning
Instructions: Read all the sentences then number them in the correct order.

Look and think.

What are Yasmin, Jack and Lee doing?

What are they thinking?

The magic carpet

Skill: Responding to reading and empathising with a character
Instructions: Look at the first picture and describe what the children are doing. Then look at the second picture and decide what the children might be thinking.

Write two lists.

Make a list of all the things Yasmin, Jack and Lee saw on their way to the North Pole.

Make a list of things to take on holiday to the North Pole.

The magic carpet

Skill: Writing in a different form - list writing
Instructions: Ask the children to look back through the story and to note the things that Yasmin, Jack and Lee saw on their way to the North Pole. Then they should write their own holiday list.

Fill in the gaps.

One day Yasmin, Jack and Lee went to the park _____ Mum. They climbed to the top _____ the tower.

'I wish this tower _____ a rocket,' said Lee.

They wished on the magic stone _____ when they opened their eyes they were _____ a rocket. They set _____ to the moon.

They landed on the moon with a _____ !

'Look _____ me,' said Lee, 'I can jump _____ high as the rocket. I'm going to look _____ moon monsters.'

'Wait for us,' shouted Jack, _____ Lee went jumping on and on.

When Yasmin looked up _____ could not see Lee.

'We had better look for _____ ,' said Yasmin.

Then Yasmin heard a noise. It was coming _____ inside a very big crater.

'It sounds _____ a monster,' said Jack.

'Quick! Let's get back to the rocket.'

'No,' said Yasmin, 'we've _____ to find Lee.'

They _____ over to the big crater. Yasmin looked inside.

There was _____ . He was laughing at them.

The children jumped _____ to the rocket but they heard the noise again. It was very, very loud.

'It _____ be a real monster,' said Lee.

Voyage into space

Skill: Reading comprehension - cloze
Instructions: Read the story carefully and then fill in each gap with a suitable word.

Put in the missing letters.

ea   or   ee

The children whispered, 'One ... two ... thr___ ...'

Lee was nowhere to be s___n.

'It must be a r___l monster,' said Lee.

'We're n___rly there,' said Yasmin.

They saw some little gr___n men.

'Let's give them something to ___t,' said Yasmin.

Jack found a sw___t in his pocket.

One Martian put a sweet on his h___d.

One Martian put a sweet in his ___r.

The Martians waved goodbye with their f___t.

Voyage into space

Skill: Phonological awareness - vowel digraphs
Instructions: Fill in the gaps with the correct vowel digraph. Then write the whole word on the line.